Home Office Research Study 251

Effects of improved street lighting on crime: a systematic review

David P. Farrington and Brandon C. Welsh

The views expressed in this report are those of the authors, not necessarily those of the Home Office (nor do they reflect Government policy).

Home Office Research, Development and Statistics Directorate
August 2002

Home Office Research Studies

The Home Office Research Studies are reports on research undertaken by or on behalf of the Home Office. They cover the range of subjects for which the Home Secretary has responsibility. Other publications produced by the Research, Development and Statistics Directorate include Findings, Statistical Bulletins and Statistical Papers.

The Research, Development and Statistics Directorate

RDS is part of the Home Office. The Home Office's purpose is to build a safe, just and tolerant society in which the rights and responsibilities of individuals, families and communities are properly balanced and the protection and security of the public are maintained.

RDS is also part of National Statistics (NS). One of the aims of NS is to inform Parliament and the citizen about the state of the nation and provide a window on the work and performance of government, allowing the impact of government policies and actions to be assessed.

Therefore –

Research Development and Statistics Directorate exists to improve policy making, decision taking and practice in support of the Home Office purpose and aims, to provide the public and Parliament with information necessary for informed debate and to publish information for future use.

First published 2002
Application for reproduction should be made to the Communication Development Unit, Room 201, Home Office, 50 Queen Anne's Gate, London SW1H 9AT.
© Crown copyright 2002   ISBN   1 84082 881 1
                           ISSN   0072 6435

This review summarises the findings of previous studies from both the USA and Britain on the effectiveness of improved street lighting on crime. Rigorous criteria were set for the inclusion of studies. These criteria were:

that improvements in street lighting were the main intervention studied;
that there was an outcome measure of crime;
that crime levels before and after the intervention were measured; and
that the studies included a comparable control area.

A meta-analysis of the eligible studies found that improved street lighting led to significant reductions in crime and with an overall reduction in recorded crime of 20 per cent across all the experimental areas.

The review assesses why street lighting has this impact on crime. The authors conclude that lighting increases community pride and confidence and strengthens informal social control and that this explains the recorded impacts, rather than increased surveillance or deterrent effects. The authors, however, suggest that these explanatory theories need to be tested more explicitly in future research and that there need to be further assessments of the impacts of different levels of illumination on crime.

The authors conclude that improvements in street lighting offer a cost-effective crime reduction measure and should be considered an important element in situational crime reduction programmes.

Carole F Willis
Head of Policing and Reducing Crime Unit

Acknowledgements

We would like to thank the following individuals for assistance in obtaining copies of evaluation reports and relevant data: Professor Norman Davidson (University of Hull), Professor Jason Ditton (University of Sheffield and Scottish Centre for Criminology), Deborah Friedman (University of Massachusetts Lowell), Professor David Griswold (Florida Atlantic University), Dr. Patrick Langan (Bureau of Justice Statistics) and Dr. Kate A. Painter (Home Office). We would also like to thank Dr. John MacLeod (Home Office) for assistance with Figure 1. Thanks also go to Professor Ross Homel, Griffith University, Australia and Dr Anthony Braga, Harvard University, USA, for acting as independent assessors for this report.

David P. Farrington
Brandon C. Welsh

David P. Farrington is Professor of Psychological Criminology in the Institute of Criminology, University of Cambridge. Brandon C. Welsh is an Assistant Professor in the Department of Criminal Justice, University of Massachusetts Lowell.

Contents

List of tables

List of figures

The main aim of this report is to present the findings of a systematic review of the effects of improved street lighting on crime. Systematic reviews of the literature use rigorous methods for locating, appraising and synthesising evidence from prior evaluation studies. They have explicit objectives, extensive searches to locate possibly relevant studies, explicit criteria for inclusion or exclusion of studies, and a structured and detailed report including methods and results sections.

There are two main theories of why improved street lighting may cause a reduction in crime. The first suggests that improved lighting leads to increased surveillance of potential offenders (both by improving visibility and by increasing the number of people on the street) and hence to the deterrence of potential offenders. The second suggests that improved lighting signals increased community investment in the area and that the area is improving, leading to increased community pride, community cohesiveness and informal social control. The first theory predicts decreases in crime especially during the hours of darkness, while the second theory predicts decreases in crime during both day-time and night-time.

The studies included

Studies were included in this review if improved lighting was the main intervention, if there was an outcome measure of crime, if there was at least one experimental area and one control area, if there were before and after measures of crime, and if the total number of crimes in each area before the intervention was at least 20.

Sixteen potentially relevant studies were obtained and screened but were excluded for various reasons, including the lack of a comparable control condition, the absence of an outcome measurement of crime and too small numbers. Most of these studies found that improved street lighting was followed by a decrease in crime.

Findings: effects of lighting on crime

Eight American evaluation studies met the criteria for inclusion in the review. Their results were mixed. Four studies found that improved street lighting was effective in reducing crime, while the other four found that it was not effective. It is not clear why the studies produced different results, although there was a tendency for "effective" studies to measure both day-time and night-time crimes and for "ineffective" studies to measure only night-time crimes. Seven of the eight evaluations were rather old, dating from the 1970s. A meta-analysis found that the 8 studies, taken together, showed that improved street lighting led to a near-significant 7 per cent decrease in crime.

Five more recent British evaluation studies met the criteria for inclusion in the review. Their results showed that improved lighting led to a significant 30 per cent decrease in crime. Furthermore, in two studies, the financial savings from reduced crimes greatly exceeded the financial costs of the improved street lighting. A meta-analysis found that the 13 studies, taken together, showed that improved lighting led to reductions in crime. The overall reduction in crime after improved lighting was 20 per cent in experimental areas compared with control areas.

Since these studies did not find that night-time crime decreased more than day-time crime, a theory of street lighting focussing on its role in increasing community pride and informal social control may be more plausible than a theory focussing on increased surveillance and increased deterrence. The results did not contradict the theory that improved lighting was most effective in reducing crime in stable homogeneous communities.

The knowledge gaps

It is recommended that future research should be designed to test the main theories of the effects of improved lighting more explicitly, and should measure crime using police records, victim surveys, and self-reports of offending. Levels of illumination, as well as crime rates, should be measured before and after the intervention in experimental and control areas. Future research should ideally include experimental, adjacent and non-adjacent control areas, in order to test hypotheses about displacement and diffusion of benefits. Ideally, a long time series of crimes before and after improved lighting in experimental and control areas should be studied. Attempts should be made to investigate how the effects of improved lighting vary according to characteristics of areas and how far there are different effects on different kinds of crimes.

Conclusion

It is concluded that improved lighting should be included as one element of a situational crime reduction programme. It is an inclusive intervention benefiting the whole of a neighbourhood and leads to an increase in perceived public safety. Improved street lighting is associated with greater use of public space and neighbourhood streets by law abiding citizens. Especially if well targeted to a high-crime area, improved street lighting can be a feasible, inexpensive and effective method of reducing crime.

1.   Background

Research on street lighting and crime

Contemporary interest in the effect of improved street lighting on crime began in North America during the dramatic rise in crime which took place in the 1960s. Many towns and cities embarked upon major street lighting programmes as a means of reducing crime, and initial results were encouraging (Wright *et al.*, 1974).

The proliferation of projects across North America led to a detailed review of the effects of street lighting on crime by Tien *et al.* (1979) as part of the National Evaluation Program of LEAA (Law Enforcement Assistance Agency) funding. Their report describes how 103 street lighting projects originally identified were eventually reduced to a final sample of only 15 that were considered by the review team to contain sufficiently rigorous evaluative information.

With regard to the impact of street lighting on crime, Tien *et al.* (1979) concluded that the results were mixed and generally inconclusive. However, each project was considered to be seriously flawed because of such problems as: weak project designs; misuse or complete absence of sound analytic techniques; inadequate measures of street lighting; poor measures of crime (all were based on police records); and insufficient appreciation of the impact of lighting on different types of crime.

Obviously, the Tien *et al.* (1979) review should have led to attempts to evaluate the effects of improved street lighting using more adequate designs and alternative measures of crime, such as victim surveys, self-reports or systematic observation. It should also have stimulated efforts to determine in what circumstances improved street lighting might lead to reductions in crime (since the desired results were obtained in some studies). Unfortunately, it was interpreted as showing that street lighting had no effect on crime and effectively killed research on the topic in the United States.

Few crime prevention initiatives could have survived the rigorous examination by Tien *et al.* (1979) unscathed. As Painter (1996) p. 318) noted:
> "Despite the fact that other National Evaluations conducted at the same time (e.g. Operation Identification, Crime Prevention Security Surveys, Citizen Patrols and Citizen Crime Reporting Projects) found evidence of programme impact to be inconsistent and inconclusive... all these strategies, with the exception of street

lighting, continued to be promoted on both sides of the Atlantic. The reasons for ignoring the potential role of street lighting are difficult to determine".

In the United Kingdom, very little research was carried out on street lighting and crime until the late 1980s (Fleming and Burrows, 1986). There was a resurgence of interest between 1988 and 1990, when three small-scale street lighting projects were implemented and evaluated in different areas of London: in Edmonton, Tower Hamlets and Hammersmith/Fulham (Painter, 1994). In each crime, disorder and fear of crime declined and pedestrian street use increased dramatically after the lighting improvements.

In contrast to these generally positive results, a major Home Office-funded evaluation in Wandsworth (Atkins *et al.*, 1991) concluded that improved street lighting had no effect on crime, and a Home Office review, published simultaneously, also asserted that "better lighting by itself has very little effect on crime" (Ramsay and Newton, 1991, p. 24). However, as further evidence accumulated, there were more signs that improved street lighting could have an effect in reducing crime. In the most recent review by Pease (1999), he considered that "the capacity of street lighting to influence crime has now been satisfactorily settled" (p. 68). He also recommended that the debate should be moved from the sterile "does it work or doesn't it?" to the more productive "how can I flexibly and imaginatively incorporate lighting in crime reduction strategy and tactics?" (p. 72).

How might improved street lighting reduce crime?

Explanations of the way street lighting improvements could prevent crime can be found in "situational" approaches which focus on reducing opportunity and increasing perceived risk through modification of the physical environment (Clarke, 1995); and in perspectives which stress the importance of strengthening informal social control and community cohesion through more effective street use (Jacobs, 1961; Angel, 1968) and investment in neighbourhood conditions (Taub *et al.*, 1984; Taylor and Gottfredson, 1986).

The situational approach to crime prevention suggests that crime can be prevented by environmental measures which directly affect offenders' perceptions of increased risks and decreased rewards. This approach is also supported by theories which emphasise natural, informal surveillance as a key to crime prevention. For example, Jacobs (1961) drew attention to the role of good visibility combined with natural surveillance as a deterrent to crime. She emphasised the association between levels of crime and public street use, suggesting that less crime would be committed in areas with an abundance of potential witnesses.

Other theoretical perspectives have emphasised the importance of investment to improve neighbourhood conditions as a means of strengthening community confidence, cohesion and social control (Wilson and Kelling, 1982; Skogan, 1990). As a highly visible sign of positive investment, improved street lighting might reduce crime if it physically improved the environment and signalled to residents that efforts were being made to invest in and improve their neighbourhood. In turn, this might lead them to have a more positive image of the area and increased community pride, optimism and cohesion. It should be noted that this theoretical perspective predicts a reduction in both day-time and night-time crime. Consequently, attempts to measure the effects of improved lighting should not concentrate purely on night-time crime.

The relationship between visibility, social surveillance and criminal opportunities is a consistently strong theme to emerge from the literature. A core assumption of both opportunity and informal social control models of prevention is that criminal opportunities and risks are influenced by environmental conditions in interaction with resident and offender characteristics. Street lighting is a tangible alteration to the built environment but it does not constitute a physical barrier to crime. However, it can act as a catalyst to stimulate crime reduction through a change in the perceptions, attitudes and behaviour of residents and potential offenders.

Causal links between street lighting and crime

It is helpful to list possible ways in which improved lighting might reduce crime (Painter and Farrington, 1999b; Pease, 1999). As mentioned, the two most popular theories focus on the deterrent effects of increased surveillance and on the effects of increased community pride on informal social control. Sample hypotheses are as follows:

- Lighting may reduce crime by improving visibility. This deters potential offenders by increasing the risks that they will be recognised or interrupted in the course of their activities (Mayhew et al., 1979). The presence of police and other authority figures also becomes more visible.

- Lighting improvements may encourage increased street usage which intensifies natural surveillance. The change in routine activity patterns works to reduce crime because it increases the flow of potentially capable guardians (Cohen and Felson, 1979). From the potential offender's perspective, the proximity of other pedestrians acts as a deterrent since the risks of being recognised or interrupted when attacking personal or property targets are increased. From the potential victim's perspective, perceived risks and fear of crime are reduced.

- Enhanced visibility and increased street usage may interact to heighten possibilities for informal surveillance. Pedestrian density and flow and surveillance have long been regarded as crucial for crime control since they can influence potential offenders' perceptions of the likely risks of being caught (Newman, 1972; Bennett and Wright, 1984).

- The renovation of a highly noticeable component of the physical environment combined with changed social dynamics may act as a psychological deterrent. Potential offenders may judge that the image of the location is improving and that social control, order, and surveillance have increased (Taylor and Gottfredson, 1986). They may deduce that crime in the relit location is riskier than elsewhere and this can influence behaviour in two ways. First, potential offenders living in the area will be deterred from committing offences or escalating their activities. Second, potential offenders from outside the area will be deterred from entering it (Wilson and Kelling, 1982). However, crimes may be displaced from the relit area to other places.

- Lighting may improve community confidence. It provides a highly noticeable sign that local authorities are investing in the fabric of the area. This offsets any previous feelings of neglect and stimulates a general "feel good" factor. It may also encourage informal social control and interventions by residents to prevent crime and disorder. Fear of crime may be reduced.

- Improved illumination may reduce fear of crime because it physically improves the environment and alters public perceptions of it. People sense that a well-lit environment is less dangerous than one that is dark (Warr, 1990). The positive image of the night-time environment in the relit area is shared by residents and pedestrians. As actual and perceived risks of victimisation lessen, the area becomes used by a wider cross-section of the community. The changed social mix and activity patterns within the locality reduce the risk and fear of crime.

It is also feasible that improved street lighting could, in certain circumstances, increase opportunities for crime. It may bring greater numbers of potential victims and potential offenders into the same physical space. Increased visibility of potential victims may allow potential offenders to make better judgements of their vulnerability and attractiveness (e.g. in terms of valuables). Increased social activity outside the home may increase the number of unoccupied homes available for burglary. Increased illumination may make it easier for offenders to commit crimes and to escape.

The effects of improved street lighting are likely to vary in different conditions. In particular, they are likely to be greater if the existing lighting is poor and if the improvement in lighting is considerable. They may vary according to characteristics of the area or the residents, the design of the area, the design of the lighting, and the places that are illuminated. For example, lighting may only improve community confidence and informal social control in relatively stable homogeneous communities, not in areas with a heterogeneous population mix and high residential mobility. The effects of improved lighting may also interact with other environmental improvements such as CCTV cameras or better locks. Improved street lighting may have different effects on different types of crimes (e.g. violence versus property) and different effects on day-time as opposed to night-time crime.

While more research is needed on the dose-response relationship between lighting and crime and on effects in different boundary conditions, the main question addressed in this review is simply whether existing evidence suggests that improved street lighting does or does not lead to reductions in crime. Therefore, it is essential in each study to produce a comparable summary measure of effect size. The main measure of effect size used here is based on changes in the number of crimes in a relit (experimental) area compared with changes in the number of crimes in a comparable control area.

Determining what works to reduce crime

Deciding what works to reduce crime requires examination of the results of prior evaluation studies whenever they are available. This is better than drawing conclusions about what works from personal experience, from anecdotal evidence, from widespread beliefs, or from a single study that was well-funded or heavily publicised. Given such advantages, it is no surprise to find that criminologists have been reviewing what works for at least 50 years. Although the methods have varied, reviewers have followed the same general set of tasks: identify and gather relevant reports of evaluation studies, assess them, and come to a summary conclusion about what works.

From the 1970s, the traditional methods used in these reviews began to be seriously criticised. One criticism focussed on the general lack of explicitness of reviews: most suffered from a lack of detail about how the reviewer conducted the research. Information was often missing about why certain studies were included while others were excluded from the review. Sometimes this lack of detail was caused by space limitations imposed on reviewers by journal or book editors. The report of the review often did not describe what literature searches were carried out in order to try to locate relevant evaluation studies. It was often difficult for the serious reader to determine how the reviewers came to their conclusions about what works. Too often, the reader was forced to accept and trust the reviewer's expertise and was not given sufficient information to permit replication of the reviewer's methods.

A second criticism focussed on the methods used. Most of the reviewers did not attempt to control problems that could potentially bias their review toward one conclusion rather than another. At its worst, a reviewer advocating a particular conclusion could selectively include only studies favouring that viewpoint in the review. For example, a reviewer in favour of street lighting could exclude evaluations that found little effect of street lighting. Such intentional distortion was fortunately rare in academic reviews (as opposed to reviews by practitioners, policy makers or others with a vested interest).

More common than intentional distortion was the failure to deal with potential biases that could compromise the results of a review. For example, some reviewers examining what works relied on easy-to-obtain journal articles as the only source for reports of evaluations. One advantage of journal articles over other documents is that they have usually passed a rigorous peer review process. However, research in other fields suggests that relying on journal articles can bias the results towards concluding that interventions are more effective than they really are. This is because researchers are more likely to submit their articles to journals when they find a positive effect of an intervention and to bury the manuscript in their file drawer when they do not. Both authors and journal editors are biased against articles reporting a null effect, sometimes falsely assuming that such papers do not contribute to knowledge.

Another criticism is that inexplicit and unsystematic review methods cannot cope with the incredible increase in research worldwide. For example, the number of journals that now publish information about crime is enormous compared to just a few years ago. Relying on journals available in a library or on articles collected in office files will no longer ensure coverage of all available studies. The internet now makes hundreds if not thousands of evaluation reports potentially accessible to prospective reviewers. In the same way that it would be difficult to make sense of a large, growing and scattered collection of police reports without orderly methods, it is also difficult to make sense of the burgeoning number of evaluation studies without some systematic method for doing so.

Characteristics of systematic reviews

In response to these criticisms, researchers began to develop and refine scientific and orderly methods for conducting reviews, and the concept of a "systematic review" arose. Individuals conducting systematic reviews use rigorous methods for locating, appraising and synthesising evidence from prior evaluation studies. Systematic reviews contain methods and results sections, and are reported with the same level of detail that characterises high quality reports of original research. Other features of systematic reviews include (see Farrington and Petrosino, 2000, 2001):

- *Explicit objectives.* The rationale for conducting the review is made clear.

- *Explicit eligibility criteria.* The reviewers specify in detail why they included certain studies and rejected others. What was the minimum level of methodological quality for inclusion? Did they consider only a particular type of evaluation design such as randomised experiments? Did the studies have to include a certain type of participant such as children or adults? What types of interventions were included? What kinds of outcome data had to be reported in the studies? All criteria or rules used in selecting eligible studies should be explicitly stated in the final report.

- *The search for studies is designed to reduce potential bias.* There are many potential ways in which bias can compromise the results of a review. The reviewers must explicitly state how they conducted their search of potential studies to reduce such bias. How did they try to locate studies reported outside scientific journals? How did they try to locate studies in foreign languages? All bibliographic databases that were searched should be made explicit so that potential gaps in coverage can be identified.

- *Each study is screened according to eligibility criteria with exclusions justified.* The searches will undoubtedly locate many citations and abstracts to potentially relevant studies. Each of the reports of these potentially relevant studies must be screened to determine if it meets the eligibility criteria for the review. A full listing of all excluded studies and the justifications for exclusion should be made available to readers.

- *Assembly of the most complete data possible.* The systematic reviewer will try to obtain all relevant evaluations meeting the eligibility criteria. In addition, all data relevant to the objectives of the review should be carefully extracted from each eligible report and coded and computerised. Sometimes, original study documents lack important information. When possible, the systematic reviewer will attempt to obtain this from the authors of the original report.

- *Quantitative techniques are used, when appropriate and possible, in analysing results.* A meta-analysis involves the statistical or quantitative analysis of the results of prior research studies. Since it involves the statistical summary of data (and especially of effect sizes), it requires a reasonable number of intervention studies that are sufficiently similar to be grouped together. A systematic review may or may not include a meta-analysis. For example, a reviewer may only find a few studies meeting the eligibility criteria. Those studies may differ just enough in the way they were conducted (e.g. in interventions or participants) to make formal meta-analysis inappropriate and potentially misleading.

- *A structured and detailed report.* The final report of a systematic review is structured and detailed so that the reader can understand each phase of the research, the decisions that were made, and the conclusions that were reached.

Aims of this report

The main aim of this report is to present the findings of a systematic review of the available research evidence on the effects of improved lighting on crime. This report is divided into four main chapters. The second chapter, on methods, reports on the criteria for inclusion of lighting studies in this review and the methods used to search for, code and analyse evaluation reports of lighting studies. In addition, it summarises studies that were obtained and screened but excluded from the review. The third chapter reports on the key features of studies that were included and the key results of each research project. The fourth and final chapter summarises the main findings and identifies research priorities and policy recommendations for the future.

2.   Methods

This report presents a systematic review of the effects of improved street lighting on crime and follows closely the methodology of this review technique. As noted above, systematic reviews use rigorous methods for locating, appraising, and synthesising evidence from prior evaluation studies, and are reported with the same level of detail that characterises high quality reports of original research. They have explicit objectives, explicit criteria for including or excluding studies, extensive searches for eligible evaluation studies from all over the world, careful extraction and coding of key features of studies, and a structured and detailed report of the methods and conclusions of the review. All of this contributes greatly to the ease of their replication by other researchers.

Criteria for inclusion of evaluation studies

In selecting programmes for inclusion in this review, the following criteria were used:

- Improved street lighting (or improved lighting) was the focus of the intervention. For programmes involving one or more other interventions, only those programmes in which improved lighting was the main intervention were included. In other cases, it would be very difficult to disentangle the effects of improved lighting from the effects of another intervention. The determination of what was the main intervention was based on the author of the report identifying it as such or, if the author did not do this, the importance the report gave to improved lighting relative to the other interventions.
- There was an outcome measure of crime. The most relevant crime outcomes were property and violent crimes.
- The evaluation design was of high quality methodologically, with the minimum design involving before and after measures in experimental and control areas (Farrington, 1997).
- There was at least one experimental area and one comparable control area.
- The total number of crimes in each area before the intervention was at least 20. The main measure of effect size was based on changes in crime rates between the before and after time periods. It was considered that a measure of change based on an N below 20 was potentially misleading. Also, any study with less than 20 crimes before would have insufficient statistical power to detect changes

in crime. The criterion of 20 is probably too low, there was reluctance to exclude studies unless their numbers were clearly inadequate.

It might perhaps be argued that the "gold standard" design should be the randomised experiment, which is the most convincing method of evaluating crime prevention programmes (Farrington, 1983). The key feature of randomised experiments is that the experimental and control groups are equated before the experimental intervention on all possible extraneous variables. Hence, any subsequent differences between them must be attributable to the intervention. The randomised experiment, however, is only the most convincing method of evaluation if a sufficiently large number of units is randomly assigned. As a rule of thumb, at least 50 units in each category are needed.

This number is relatively easy to achieve with individuals but very difficult to achieve with larger units such as areas, as in improved street lighting programmes. Sherman and Weisburd (1995) were able to allocate 110 high crime places (about the size of a street block) at random either to receive increased police patrolling or not, but it is hard to see how this approach could be used in practice with street lighting. For example, new cables would have to be laid all over a city to improve the lighting of a few blocks chosen at random.

For larger units such as areas, the best and most feasible design usually involves before and after measures in experimental and control conditions together with statistical control of extraneous variables. This is the best way of dealing with the following threats to internal validity (Cook and Campbell, 1979; Painter and Farrington, 1997, p. 212):

- *History:* decreases in crime after improved lighting might be caused by other changes over time (e.g. decreased unemployment rates);

- *Trends:* decreases in crime after improved lighting might be attributable to a continuation of pre-existing trends;

- *Measurement:* decreases in crime after improved lighting might be attributable to changes in methods of measurement (e.g. police recording practices);

- *Regression:* decreases in crime after improved lighting might be attributable to a fluctuation downwards following an unusually high crime rate period.

The statistical control of extraneous variables influencing crime rates can deal with selection effects due to prior differences between experimental and control areas.

In general, if crime decreases in an experimental area after an intervention, it is difficult to be sure that the decrease was caused by the intervention without being able to compare crime trends in the experimental area with crime trends in a comparable control area.

Search strategies

The following four search strategies were used to identify evaluations of improved lighting programmes meeting the criteria for inclusion in this review:

- searches of on-line databases (see below)
- searches of reviews of the literature on the effects of improved lighting on crime (for a list of reviews consulted, see Appendix 1)
- searches of bibliographies of evaluation reports of improved lighting studies
- contacts with leading researchers (see Acknowledgements).

Both published and unpublished reports were considered in these searches. Furthermore, the searches were international in scope and were not limited to the English language. These searches were completed in January 2001 and reflect material published or reported up to the end of 2000.

The following eight databases were searched:
- Criminal Justice Abstracts
- National Criminal Justice Reference Service (NCJRS) Abstracts
- Sociological Abstracts
- Social Science Abstracts (SocialSciAbs)
- Educational Resources Information Clearinghouse (ERIC)
- Government Publications Office Monthly Catalogue (GPO Monthly)
- Psychology Information (PsychInfo)
- Public Affairs Information Service (PAIS) International.

These databases were selected on the basis of the most comprehensive coverage of criminological, criminal justice and social science literatures. They are also among the top databases recommended by the Crime and Justice Group of the Campbell Collaboration, and other systematic reviews of interventions in the field of crime and justice have used them (e.g. Petrosino *et al.*, 2000).

The following terms were used to search the eight databases noted above: street lighting, lighting, illumination and natural surveillance. When applicable, "crime" was then added to each of these terms (e.g. street lighting and crime) to narrow the search parameters.

Only studies that might potentially be included in the review were sought. As already mentioned, the exhaustive review by Tien *et al.* (1979) identified 103 street lighting projects carried out in the 1970s but only considered that 15 (listed on pp. 51-54) met their minimum methodological standards. Attempts were made to obtain 11 of these 15 evaluation reports. For the other four studies (conducted in Baltimore, Chicago, Richmond/Virginia and Washington DC), Tien *et al.* (1979) could not determine from the report that there was any kind of experimental-control comparison. Hence, attempts were not made to obtain and screen every possible study on lighting and crime conducted prior to Tien *et al.* (1979), only studies that conceivably might meet the criteria for inclusion. Attempts were made to obtain and screen every possible study conducted after the review by Tien *et al.* (1979).

These search strategies resulted in the collection of 13 evaluations of improved lighting programmes that met the criteria for inclusion in this review. A few of the identified evaluations, which may or may not have met the criteria for inclusion, could not be obtained. The (unpublished) reports of these programmes are listed in Appendix 2.

Programmes not meeting inclusion criteria

In the searches for evaluations of improved lighting programmes, several of those obtained and screened did not meet the criteria for inclusion and thus have not been included in the present review. Altogether, 16 improved lighting programmes were excluded. Table 2.1 lists these programmes and identifies the main reasons for their exclusion. There are two main reasons for listing these studies. First, this conforms with the widespread practice in systematic reviews of identifying and summarising excluded studies. Second, it allows readers to judge for themselves the strength of the observed effects of lighting on crime in excluded compared with included studies in light of the methodological differences between the studies.

As shown in Table 2.1, 11 evaluations were excluded because they did not use a comparable control area in assessing the impact of the improved street lighting intervention, and two because the number of crimes was too small. Two evaluations were excluded because they did not include crime as an outcome measure, and one (Nair *et al.*, 1993)

Table 2.1: *Street lighting evaluations not meeting inclusion criteria*

Author, Publication Date, and Location	Reason for Not Including Programme	Other Interventions	Sample Size	Follow-up and Result
Hack (1974), Norfolk, Virginia, USA	Crime not measured (fear of crime measured)	None	n/a	n/a
Siemon and Vardell (1974), Dade County, Florida, USA	No control area used	None	1 public housing project (Larchmont Gardens)	9 months; class I crimes: -22.9% (245 to 189); class II crimes: - 51.4% (72 to 35)
Krause (1977), New Orleans, Louisiana, USA	No control area used	None	1 commercial area	9 months; commercial nighttime burglary (mean monthly difference): - 1.4
Kushmuk and Whittemore (1981), Griswold (1984), Lavrakas and Kushmuk (1986), Portland, Oregon, USA	Non-comparable control area (rest of city)	Multiple (e.g. security surveys, clean-up days)	1 commercial strip and adjacent streets	34 months; commercial burglary decreased, other crimes no change (time series analysis)
Bachner (1985), Camillus, New York, USA	No control area used	None	1 parking lot of shopping mall	<1 year; vehicle break-ins: "virtually eliminated"
Davidson and Goodey (1991), Hull, England	No control area used	None	1 residential area (Dukeries)	6 weeks; percentage of victimisations: +9.5% (63% to 69%)

Study	Notes	Other interventions	Areas / units	Results
Vrij and Winkel (1991), Enkhuizen, The Netherlands	Crime not measured (fear of crime and perceived risk of victimisation measured)a	None	n/a	n/a
Atkins, Husain and Storey (1991), Wandsworth, England	Number of crimes too small. Victim survey response rate before = 37%	None	1 relit area, 1 adjacent non-relit area	12 months: Reported crime: -14.5% (7480 to 6399) VS: 7 weeks: relit crimes -35.9% (39 decrease to 25); control crimes -69.2% (13 to 4).
Ramsay and Newton (1991), Hastings, England	Number of crimes too small	None	1 relit area, 1 control area	7 months: Recorded crime in relit area + 40.0% (15 to 21); control crimes + 30.6% (85 to 111).
Challinger (1992), South Australia and Northern Territory, Australia	No control area used	Multiple (e.g., target hardening, security staff)	35,000 public pay phones	3 years;b vandalism: -19.0% (1,373 to 1,112)
Nair, Ditton, and Phillips (1993), Glasgow, Scotland	No control area used and crime not measured (fear of crime measured)	Multiple (e.g., paths widened, entry phones)	n/a	n/a
Tilley (1993), Salford, England	No control area used	None	3 businesses	12 months; total crimes: - 72.4% (29 to 8)
La Vigne (1994), Austin, Texas, USA	No control area used	None	38 convenience stores	n/a.; thefts of gasoline: - 65%

Ditton and Nair (1994), Glasgow and High Blantyre, Scotland	No control area used	None	1 residential area in both sites	3 months; 2 sites combined: total personal victimisation: -50.0% (12 to 6); total vehicle victimisation: -95.7% (23 to 1); total police-recorded crime: -14.0% (57 to 49)
Painter (1994), 3 areas in London, England — Edmonton	No control area used (for all 3 sites)	None (for all 3 sites)	1 street and 1 pedestrian footpath	6 weeks; total crime (at night): -85.7% (21 to 3)
Tower Hamlets			1 street	6 weeks; total crime (at night): -77.8% (18 to 4)
Hammersmith and Fulham			1 street	12 months; total crime (at night): 2 to 0
Nair, McNair, and Ditton (1997), Glasgow, Scotland	No control area used	None	1 carriage-way	2 years; pestering/following: -48.2% (112 to 58); sexual proposition: -54.2% (24 to 11); assault/mugging: 3 to 1; sexual assault: 1 to 0 (all at night)

a Respectively, the questions asked were: "To what extent do you feel safe here?" and "How likely do you think it is that you could be molested here?" (Vrij & Winkel, 1991, p. 211).

b Follow-up period not specified for street lighting intervention. Notes: n/a. = not available or not applicable. VS = Victim Survey.

was excluded because it neither had a control area nor an outcome measure of crime. Three of these programmes also included other interventions, making it difficult to disentangle the effects of the improved lighting from the effects of the other interventions.

For example, Atkins et al. (1991) first carried out an analysis of reported crimes in a relit area before and after the improved street lighting, and found that crime decreased by 14.5 per cent after. This analysis was excluded because it did not study reported crimes in a control area. Then a victim survey was carried out in experimental and control areas before and after the improved lighting. Unfortunately, this was problematic because of the low response rate (37% before) and the short time periods covered (only seven weeks before and after). This evaluation was excluded because of small numbers and inadequate statistical power to detect effects; the number of crimes in the control area in the pretest was only 13. The Hastings evaluation by Ramsay and Newton (1991) was also excluded because the number of crimes in the relit area in the pretest was less than 20. Several of the other excluded programmes listed in Table 2.1 had short follow-up periods (less than one year) and were limited by small numbers of crimes.

The Portland (Oregon) evaluation of Kushmuk and Whittemore (1981), Griswold (1984) and Lavrakas and Kushmuk (1986) was methodologically sophisticated in many ways but was problematic for two main reasons. First, the experimental area (a 3.5-mile long commercial strip called the Union Avenue Corridor) was compared with the rest of the city of Portland:

> "An inherent weakness of the evaluation design used to study CPTED [Crime Prevention Through Environmental Design] was the lack of a "control group" with which to compare findings on the UAC [Union Avenue Corridor]. The evaluators were keenly aware of the internal validity problems caused by the lack of a non-equivalent control site – most notably, the difficulty in separating out the effects of historical events from program effects. In the early stages of this study, attempts were made to identify a comparable control site in Portland, but this proved impossible. It was discovered that Union Avenue was unique as a commercial area, especially in regards to its combination of racial make-up and social/economic factors. Given these circumstances, the decision was made to use city-wide crime data as a control. By using a city-wide index of crime, the evaluation was able to determine if crime changes observed on the UAC were unique to that area, and, therefore, attributable to CPTED activities" (Kushmuk and Whittemore, 1981, p. 15).

Second, it was impossible to disentangle the effects of the improved street lighting from the effects of other interventions that were implemented at the same time, in particular security surveys (where security advisors gave people recommendations about target hardening techniques) and community events such as "clean-up days".

The reports did not provide raw data that would enable calculation of numbers of crimes before and after the intervention, but this information was kindly provided by Professor David Griswold. The most relevant comparison is between 1975 (the last full year before the intervention) and 1978 (the first full year after the intervention). Between these years, commercial burglary decreased by 59 per cent in the experimental area, compared with a 26 per cent decrease in the remainder of the city, a significant difference (odds ratio = 1.83, p<.0001; see later for a discussion of the odds ratio).

Between these years, residential burglary decreased by 40 per cent in the experimental area, compared with a 20 per cent decrease in the remainder of the city, a significant difference (odds ratio = 1.34, p = .002). Commercial robbery decreased by 29 per cent in the experimental area, compared with a 6 per cent decrease in the remainder of the city, but this effect was not significant because of small numbers (odds ratio = 1.33). Street crime decreased by 6 per cent in the experimental area, compared with a 30 per cent increase in the remainder of the city, a significant difference (odds ratio = 1.39, p<.0001). Therefore, the results of these analyses are more positive than the conclusions drawn by the researchers from the time series analyses. In total, between 1975 and 1978, all of these types of crimes decreased by 28 per cent in the experimental area, compared with a 6 per cent decrease in the remainder of the city, a significant difference (odds ratio = 1.30, p<.0001).

Most of the excluded studies found that crimes decreased after improved street lighting in an experimental area: Siemon and Vardell (1974), Krause (1977), Griswold (1984), Bachner (1985), Atkins et al. (1991), Challinger (1992), Tilley (1993), Ditton and Nair (1994), La Vigne (1994), Painter (1994, three studies) and Nair et al. (1997). In contrast, Davidson and Goodey (1991) and Ramsay and Newton (1991) found that crimes increased after improved street lighting. Therefore on the basis of "head counting", these studies show that improved lighting is followed by decreases in crime. However, it is unclear how many of these changes were statistically significant. The low level of internal validity of these studies (together with other methodological problems) means that too much weight cannot be given to the results.

3.   Results

Key features of evaluations

Tables 3.1 and 3.2 summarise key features of the eight American lighting evaluations that were included in the review, while Tables 3.4 and 3.5 summarise key features of five British lighting evaluations that were included. The programmes are listed in chronological order, according to the date of publication. Tables 3.1 and 3.4 list the following features:

- *Author, publication date and location:* The authors and dates of the most relevant evaluation reports are listed here, along with the location of the programme.

- *Context of intervention:* The physical setting in which the improved lighting intervention took place.

- *Type of intervention and other interventions:* The intervention is identified together with the increase in lighting intensity (where known). Any other concurrent interventions are noted.

- *Sample size:* The number and any special features of the experimental and control areas are identified.

- *Outcome measure and data source:* As noted above, crime was the outcome measure of interest in this review. Here the specific crime types as well as the data source of the outcome measure are identified.

- *Research design:* As noted above, the minimum research design for a programme to be included in this review involves before and after measures in experimental and comparable control areas. Information about non-comparable control areas (e.g. the remainder of the city) is not included. The lengths of the before and after time periods of the evaluation are also noted here.

Tables 3.2 and 3.5 list the most important results. In summarising results, the focus was on the most relevant crime outcomes for this review (i.e. property and violent crimes) and on before and after comparisons in experimental and control areas. Data were amalgamated where possible and appropriate. For example, two experimental areas would be combined, as would two control areas. As far as possible, the percentage change in crime after the improved lighting compared with before was reported in Tables 3.2 and 3.5. The numbers of crimes in experimental and control areas in the pretest were also listed in light of the requirement that the minimum number of crimes before in each area should be 20. The American minimum was 49 (Indianapolis), while the British minimum was 43 (Dover).

Evaluations of improved lighting programmes differ on many different dimensions, and it is impossible to include more than a few in summary tables. Two important issues that are not often addressed adequately are displacement and diffusion of benefits. Displacement is often defined as the unintended increase in crime following a crime reduction scheme; for a discussion of "benign" or desirable effects of displacement, see Barr and Pease (1990). Five different forms of displacement have been identified by Reppetto (1976): temporal (change in time), tactical (change in method), target (change in victim), territorial (change in place), and functional (change in type of crime). Diffusion of benefits is defined as the unintended decrease in crime following a crime reduction scheme, or the "complete reverse" of displacement (Clarke and Weisburd, 1994).

In order to investigate territorial displacement and diffusion of benefits, the minimum design involves one experimental area, one adjacent area, and one non-adjacent control area. If crime decreased in the experimental area, increased in the adjacent area, and stayed constant in the control area, this might be evidence of displacement. If crime decreased in the experimental and adjacent areas and stayed constant or increased in the control area, this might be evidence of diffusion of benefits. Few studies in the tables included both adjacent and non-adjacent but comparable control areas. More had an adjacent control area and the remainder of the city as another control area. Results obtained in the remainder of the city were not included in the tables because the remainder of the city was not comparable to the experimental area.

In many cases, the experimental area was chosen for relighting because it was a high crime area. This raises the problem of "regression to the mean"; an area which is high at one time is likely to decrease at a later time. In order to investigate this, longtime-series of crimes before and after the intervention in experimental and control areas are needed.

Results of American studies

Table 3.1:   American street lighting evaluations meeting inclusion criteria

Author, Publication Date, Location	Context of Intervention	Type of Intervention (Other interventions)	Sample Size	Outcome Measure and Data source	Research Design
1.Atlanta Regional Commission (1974) Atlanta, Georgia	City centre (high robbery)	Improved (4x) street lighting (none)	E=selected streets in census tract 27, C=rest of streets in census tract 27	Crime (robbery, assault, and burglary); police records	Before-after, experimental-control; Before and after periods = 12 months
2.Department of Inter-governmental Fiscal Liaison (1973, 1974), Milwaukee, Wisconsin	Residential and commercial area (older residents)	Improved (7x) street lighting (none)	E=1 area (3.5 miles of streets), C=1 adjacent area	Crime (property and person categories); police records	Before-after, experimental-control; Before and after periods = 12 months
3.Inskeep and Goff (1974), Portland, Oregon	Residential neighbourhood (high crime)	Improved (2x) street lighting (none)	2 E areas, 2 A areas, C= surrounding areas	Crime (robbery, assault, and burglary); police records	Before-after, experimental-control; Before and after periods = 6 or 11 months
4. Wright et al. (1974), Kansas City, Missouri	Residential and commercial areas (high crime)	Improved street lighting (none)	E=129 relit blocks in 4 relit areas, C=600 non-relit blocks in same areas	Crime (violent and property offences); police records	Before-after, experimental-control; Before and after periods = 12 months

Study	Context	Intervention	Design	Outcome measure	Evaluation design
5. Harrisburg Police Department (1976), Harrisburg, Pennsylvania	Residential neighbourhood	Improved street lighting (none)	E=1 high crime area, C=1 adjacent area	Crime (violent and property offences); police records	Before-after, experimental-control; Before and after periods = 12 months
6. Sternhell (1977), New Orleans, Louisiana	Residential and commercial areas	Improved street lighting (none)	E=2 high crime areas, C=2 adjacent areas	Crime (burglary, vehicle theft, and assault); police records	Before-after, experimental-control; Before period = 51 months; after period = 29 months
7. Lewis and Sullivan (1979), Fort Worth, Texas	Residential neighbourhood	Improved (3x) street lighting (none)	E = 1 high crime area, C = 1 adjacent area	Crime (total); police records Before and after	Before-after, experimental-control; periods = 12 months
8. Quinet and Nunn (1998), Indianapolis, Indiana	Residential neighbourhood	Improved street lighting (police initiatives)	E=2 multi-block areas, C=2 areas with no new lights	Calls for service (violent and property crime); police records	Before-after, experimental-control; Before and after period = 6 - 9 months

Notes: E = Experimental, A = adjacent, C = control, 4X = 4 times increase in lighting (etc.)

Table 3.2: Results of American street lighting evaluations

Study	All Crimes (E Before, C Before)	Types of Crimes	Conclusions
1. Atlanta	T: E+ 32.5%, C+ 84.2% N: E+ 88.7%, C+ 121.5% D: E-16.4%, C+ 33.3% (114, 234)	Rob: E- 8.1%, C+ 23.6% Ast: E+ 418.2%, C+ 319.6% Burg: E- 9.8%, C+ 32.8%	Effective
2. Milwaukee	T (7m): E- 5.6%, C+ 29.2% N (12m): E- 5.9%, C - 1.7% D (7m): E+ 2.2%, C+ 37.0% (161, 370)	Prop (N): E- 5.8%, C- 3.3% Viol (N): E- 6.3%, C+ 2.0%	Effective
3. Portland	N: E- 6.5%, A - 11.8%, C - 12.0% (340,1011; A Before = 365)	Rob (N): E- 31.5%, A- 36.6% C- 30.3% Ast (N) E-11.3%, A- 22.1%, C- 5.6% Burg (N): E+ 11.9%, A+ 11.6%, C - 7.3%	Not effective
4. Kansas City	N: E - 36.7%, C- 21.2% (188, 386)	Rob (N): E- 52.2%, C-16.9% Ast (N): E-40.5%, C+ 3.8% Larc (N): E- 39.2%, C-28.9% MVT (N): E+ 3.0%, C- 34.1%	Effective for violence
5. Harrisburg	N: E+ 14.4%, C+ 17.1% (201, 117)	Rob N): E-8.7%, C+ 7.1% Ast (N): E+ 9.4%, C- 24.2% Burg (N): E+ 32.9%, C+46.0% MVT (N): E+ 2.4%, C+ 20.0%	Not effective
6. New Orleans	N: E - 25.2%, C- 26.4% (1519, 1163)	Ast (N): E-18.8%, C- 30.1% Burg (N): E- 25.8%, C- 28.8% MVT (N): E- 29.0%, C- 22.6%	Not effective
7. Fort Worth	E - 21.5%, C+ 8.8% (261, 80)		Effective

| 8. Indianapolis | E+ 39.0%, C+ 4.1% (Excluding police actions) (118, 49) | Viol: E+ 39.2%, C+ 81.6% Prop: E-13.8%, C- 18.2% (including police actions) | Not effective |

Notes:
T = Total, N = Night, D = Day
E = Experimental, A = Adjacent, C = Control
Rob = Robbery, Ast = Assault, Burg = Burglary
Prop = Property, Viol = Violence, larc = Larceny
MVT = Motor vehicle theft
E Before = No. of crimes in Experimental area before
C Before = No. of crimes in Control area before

Tables 3.1 and 3.2 summarise key features of the eight American studies that were considered to meet our minimum methodological standards. Only the last two studies (Fort Worth and Indianapolis) were published, but their methodological quality was not higher than that of the first six studies. Only the most relevant comparisons are shown in the tables. For example, the Indianapolis study included a second experimental area and a second control area, but calls for service to the police were very low in these areas (e.g. only 10 in the experimental area in the before time period), so they are not included in the tables. Also in this study, there were some police initiatives (involving increased police presence) that generated calls for service. Where possible, the dates of these were excluded from the analysis.

In general, the experimental area was chosen for relighting because it had a high crime rate or was otherwise problematic. Only four of the eight evaluations specified the degree of improvement in the lighting: by seven times in Milwaukee, four times in Atlanta, three times in Fort Worth, and two times in Portland. However, the description of the lighting in other cases (e.g. "high intensity street lighting" in Harrisburg and New Orleans) suggests that there was a marked improvement in the degree of illumination. Only in Indianapolis was the improved street lighting confounded with another concurrent intervention (as explained above), and it was sometimes possible to disentangle this.

The control area was often adjacent to the experimental area. Hence, similar decreases in crime in experimental and control areas could reflect diffusion of benefits rather than no effects of lighting. In most cases, the reports noted that the control area was similar to the experimental area in socio-demographic factors or crime rates. However, none of the evaluations attempted to control for any prior non-comparability of experimental and control areas. Only one evaluation (Portland) included an adjacent area and a comparable non-adjacent control area, but it found no effect of improved lighting.

The outcome measure of crime was always based on police records before and after the improved street lighting. All evaluations except Fort Worth also provided comparable before and after data on types of crimes. The Indianapolis evaluation was based on calls for service to the police, many of which did not clearly involve crimes (e.g. calls for "disturbance"). Only the Atlanta and Milwaukee studies provided total, night-time and day-time crimes. The Portland, Kansas City, Harrisburg and New Orleans studies measured only night-time crimes and the Fort Worth and Indianapolis studies reported only total crimes.

The before and after time periods were sometimes different for different comparisons. In Milwaukee, for example, night-time data were provided for 12 months before and after, but day-time and total data were provided only for seven months before and after. The New

Orleans evaluation had different time periods before (51 months) and after (29 months) but reported average monthly crime rates. Similarly, the Indianapolis evaluation reported average weekly calls for service.

Table 3.2 summarises the key results. In four evaluations the improved street lighting was considered to be effective in reducing crime (Atlanta, Milwaukee, Fort Worth and – for violence – Kansas City). In the other four evaluations, the improved street lighting was considered to be ineffective (Portland, Harrisburg, New Orleans and Indianapolis).

Improved street lighting was most clearly effective in reducing crime in the Fort Worth evaluation. Crimes decreased by 21.5 per cent in the experimental area and increased by 8.8 per cent in the control area (Lewis and Sullivan, 1979, p.75). Since crime in the whole city stayed constant (a decrease of 1.1%), it might be argued that some crime had been displaced from the experimental to the adjacent control area. In the experimental area, property crimes decreased but violent crimes did not. Information about types of crime was not provided for the control area, and information was not provided about night-time as opposed to day-time crime.

Improved street lighting was followed by a decrease in robberies and burglaries in Atlanta, whereas the incidence of these crimes increased in the control area (Atlanta Regional Commission, 1974, pp. 11-12). There was an increase in assaults in the experimental area, but the numbers were relatively small (from 11 to 57). Overall, day-time crime decreased by 16.4 per cent in the experimental area after the improved lighting, in comparison with an increase of 33.3 per cent in the control area. Night-time crime increased considerably in both areas.

In Milwaukee, information about total crimes was only available for seven months before and after the improved lighting. Impressively, crimes decreased by 5.6 per cent in the experimental area and increased by 29.2 per cent in the control area (Department of Intergovernmental Fiscal Liaison, 1973, p. 6). Similar results were obtained for night-time crimes (15.3% decrease in experimental area, 20.0% increase in control area). There was also a big effect on day-time crimes (2.2% increase in experimental area, 37.0% increase in control area). However, the effects were much less in a later report (Department of Intergovernmental Fiscal Liaison, 1974, p. 3) covering 12 months before and after for night-time crimes only (5.9% decrease in experimental area, 1.7% decrease in control area).

In Kansas City, improved street lighting was effective in reducing night-time violent crimes (robbery and assault) but not night-time property crimes (larceny and motor vehicle theft). Violent crimes decreased by 51.9 per cent in the experimental area, compared with 7.2 per cent in the control area (Wright *et al.*, 1974, p. 49). However, property crimes decreased more in the control area (32.0%) than in the experimental area (22.6%). These results were statistically significant for violent crimes but not for property crimes.

In Indianapolis, the results were difficult to interpret. When the dates of special police initiatives were excluded, crimes increased more in the experimental area than in the control area (Quinet and Nunn, 1998, pp. 759 and 763; their experimental areas A and C are included in this report's analyses). However, the data on types of crimes, which did not exclude these dates, showed that violent crimes increased more in the control area (Quinet and Nunn, 1998, pp. 769 and 773). The data on types of crimes are more interesting because unlike total calls for service they clearly refer to crimes. However, they are severely limited by small numbers.

In Portland, there was little evidence that improved street lighting had led to any reduction in night-time crime. The analysis of this project was complicated by the fact that one set of experimental, adjacent and control areas was followed up for 11 months before and after, while another set was followed up for six months before and after (Inskeep and Goff, 1974, p. 10). The figures are combined in Table 3.2. In general, changes in crime in the experimental areas were similar to and not more desirable than changes in crime in the adjacent and control areas. Therefore, there was no evidence in favour of either a crime-reducing effect of improved lighting or a diffusion of benefits to adjacent areas.

Finally, in Harrisburg night-time crimes increased similarly in experimental and control areas (Harrisburg Police Department, 1976, Tables 1 and 2); and in New Orleans night-time crimes decreased similarly in experimental and control areas (Sternhell, 1977, pp. 13-15).

Why was improved street lighting effective in reducing crime in some studies but not in others? There was no clear tendency for some types of crime (e.g. violence) to decrease more than others. One clear difference was that both day-time and night-time crimes were measured in the "effective" evaluations (Atlanta, Milwaukee and Fort Worth), whereas only night-time crimes were measured in the "ineffective" evaluations (Portland, Harrisburg and New Orleans). However, both day-time and night-time crimes were measured in the Indianapolis evaluation. "Night-time" was not defined in Portland or New Orleans; in Harrisburg, it was defined as the hours between 8.00 p.m. and 4.00 a.m., so this would exclude some crimes committed during the hours of darkness.

Table 3.3:   Meta-analysis of American street lighting evaluations (odds ratios)

	Total	Violence	Property
1. Atlanta	1.39 **	1.30	1.47
2. Milwaukee	1.37 **	1.09	1.03
3. Portland (N)	0.94	1.04	0.83
4. Kansas City (N)	1.24	1.79 **	0.88
5. Harrisburg (N)	1.02	0.81	1.14
6. New Orleans (N)	1.01	0.86	1.07
7. Fort Worth	1.38 *	..	..
8. Indianapolis	0.75	..	..
Total	1.08 *	1.07	1.02

Note: The odds ratio indicates the change in crimes in the control area divided by the change in crimes in the
       experimental area. Odds ratios greater than 1.0 indicate a desirable effect of improved lighting.
       ** p<.05. * p<.10.
       (N) = Available for night only.
       .. = Not available for Fort Worth; N too small (less than 10 before) for Indianapolis.

Table 3.3 presents the results of a meta-analysis of the eight American projects. In order to carry out a meta-analysis, a comparable measure of effect size is needed in each project. This has to be based on the number of crimes in experimental and control areas before and after the intervention, because this is the only information that is regularly provided in these evaluations. Here, the odds ratio is used as the measure of effect size. For example, in Atlanta, the odds of a crime after given a crime before in the control area were (431/234) or 1.842. The odds of a crime after given a crime before in the experimental area were (151/114) or 1.325. The odds ratio therefore was (1.842/1.325) or 1.39. This was statistically significant (z = 2.22, p = .026, two-tailed).

The odds ratio has a very simple and meaningful interpretation. It indicates the proportional change in crime in the control area compared with the experimental area. An odds ratio greater than 1.0 indicates a desirable effect of improved lighting, while an odds ratio less than 1.0 indicates an undesirable effect. In this example, the odds ratio of 1.39 indicates that crime increased by 39 per cent in the control area compared with the experimental area. An odds ratio of 1.39 could also indicate that crime decreased by 28 per cent in the experimental area compared with the control area, since the change in the experimental area compared with the control area is the inverse of the odds ratio, or (1/1.39) here.

The odds ratios confirm this report's previous conclusions. Total crimes reduced significantly after improved street lighting in Atlanta and Milwaukee, and nearly significantly in Fort Worth. Violent crimes reduced significantly in Kansas City. No other effect sizes were significant.

Perhaps the most interesting and unexpected result occurred when the odds ratios from the eight studies were combined using the methods recommended by Lipsey and Wilson (2001, p. 130). These require that each effect size has a known standard error, which is true for the odds ratio. (This was one reason for choosing to use the odds ratio.) The average effect size (weighted according to the standard error of each study) was an odds ratio of 1.08, but this was nearly significant ($z = 1.85$, $p = .064$). Thus, pooling the data from these eight studies, there was some evidence that improved street lighting led to a reduction in crime. Overall, crime increased by 8 per cent in control areas compared with experimental areas, or conversely crime decreased by 7 per cent in experimental areas compared with control areas.

The 8 effect sizes were significantly variable ($Q = 14.81$, 7 d.f., $p = .039$). This means that they were not randomly distributed around the average effect size. The key dimension on which they differed seemed to be whether they were based on data for both night and day (Atlanta, Milwaukee, Fort Worth and Indianapolis) or for night only (the other four studies). For the four night/day studies, the average effect size was an odds ratio of 1.28 ($z = 3.05$, $p = .002$), meaning that crime increased by 28 per cent in control areas compared with experimental areas ($Q = 6.02$, 3 d.f., n.s., so no evidence of heterogeneity of these four studies). For the four night only studies, odds ratio = 1.02 (n.s.), indicating a negligible effect on crime, and $Q = 2.81$ (3 d.f., n.s.), again indicating homogeneity. Therefore, the eight American studies could be divided into two blocks of four, one block showing that crime reduced after improved street lighting and the other block showing that it did not. Surprisingly, evidence of a reduction in crime was only obtained when both day-time and night-time crimes were measured, although this feature may be a proxy for some other feature of the different evaluation studies.

Unfortunately, all the American evaluations (except the Indianapolis one) are now rather dated, since they were all carried out in the 1970s. More recent American evaluations of the effect of improved street lighting need to be conducted. The British evaluations, on the other hand were all published in the 1990s.

Results of British studies

Table 3.4:   British street lighting evaluations meeting inclusion criteria

Author, Publication Date, Location	Context of Intervention	Type of Intervention (Other Interventions)	Sample Size	Outcome Measure and Data Source	Research Design
1. Poyner (1991) Dover	Parking garage (in town centre)	Improved lighting (at main entrance/ exit); (Fencing, office constructed)	E = 1 parking garage C=2 open parking lots close to E	Crime (total and theft of and from vehicles); police records	Before-after, experimental-control; Before and after periods = 24 months
2. Shaftoe (1994) Bristol	Residential neighbourhood	Improved (2x) street lighting; (none)	E = 2 police beats C=2 adjacent police beats	Crime (total); police records	Before-after, experimental-control; Before and after periods = 12 months
3. Poyner and Webb (1997) Birmingham	City-centre market	Improved lighting (none)	E=1 market C=2 markets	Thefts; police records	Before-after, experimental-control; Before and after periods = 12 months (6 months in each of 2 years)
4. Painter and Farrington (1997, 2001a), Dudley	Local authority housing estate	Improved (2x) street lighting (none)	E=1 housing estate C=1 adjacent estate	Crime (total and types of offences); victim survey and self-reports	Before-after, experimental-control and statistical analyses; Before and after periods = 12 months
5. Painter and Farrington (1999b) Stoke-on-Trent	Local authority housing estate	Improved (5x) street lighting (none)	E=1 housing estate A=2 adjacent estates C=2 non-adjacent estates	Crime (total and types of offences); victim survey	Before-after, experimental-control and statistical analyses; Before and after periods = 12 months

Notes: E = Experimental, A = Adjacent, C = Control. 2x = two times increase (etc.)

Table 3.5: **Results of British street lighting evaluations**

Study	All Crimes (E Before, C Before)	Types of Crimes	Conclusions
1. Dover	E- 49.0%, C- 41.9% (96, 43)	TFV: E- 21.4%, C- 50.0%; TOV: E- 81.6%, C- 47.1%	Effective (theft of vehicles)
2. Bristol	T: E-5.3%, C+ 27.8% N: E- 5.8%, C+ 19.3% D: E- 4.9%, C+ 33.3% (2931, 1315)	Rob (N): E+ 50.8%, C- 27.8%; TFV (N): E- 29.6%, C+ 10.8%	Effective
3. Birmingham	(136, 81)	Theft (D): E- 78.7%, C- 18.5%	Effective
4. Dudley	VS: E- 40.8%, C - 15.0% SR: E - 35.0%, C- 14.0% N: E- 31.9%, C- 2.0% D: E- 38.7%, C- 26.0% (VS 495, 368) (SR 480, 499)	VS Burg: E- 37.7%, C- 13.4% Veh: E- 49.1%, C- 15.7% Viol: E- 40.8%, C+ 4.9% SR Viol: E- 39.6%, C- 25.6% Vand: E- 18.2%, C+ 10.9% Dish: E- 7.1%, C+ 60.0%	Effective
5. Stoke-on-Trent	VS: E- 42.9%, A- 45.4%, C- 2.0% (551, 61: A Before = 243)	VS Burg: E- 15.1%, A- 20.3%, C+ 0.6% Veh: E- 46.4%, A- 47.7%, C- 34.7% Viol: E- 68.0%, A- 66.3%, C- 39.2%	Effective

Note: E = Experimental, A = Adjacent, C = Control
T = Total, N = Night, D = Day
VS = Victim survey, SR = Self-reports
TFV = Theft from vehicle, TOV = Theft of vehicle
Rob = Robbery, Burg = Burglary
Veh = Vehicle crime, Viol = Violence, Vand = Vandalism
Dish = Dishonesty
E Before = No. of crimes in Experimental area before
C Before = No. of crimes in Control area before

Tables 3.4 and 3.5 summarise key features of the five British studies that were considered to meet the minimum methodological standards. All were published. The improved lighting interventions occurred in a variety of settings, including a parking garage and a market as well as residential neighbourhoods. Three of the evaluations specified the degree of improvement in lighting: by five times in Stoke and by two times in Bristol (approximately) and Dudley. Control areas were usually located close to experimental areas.

The outcome measure of crime was based on police records for three studies and on victim surveys in the other two cases (in Dudley and Stoke). Uniquely, the Dudley project also evaluated the impact of improved street lighting using self-reported delinquency surveys of young people. This project also included self-reports of victimisation of young people and measures of fear of crime (Painter and Farrington, 2001a). Table 3.5 shows that improved lighting was considered to be effective in reducing crime in four studies (Bristol, Birmingham, Dudley and Stoke).

In the fifth (Dover) study, the improved lighting was confounded with other improvements, including fencing to restrict access to the parking garage and the construction of an office near the main entrance. On the basis of police records, Poyner (1991) concluded that the intervention had reduced thefts of vehicles but not thefts from vehicles. It was also considered that the crime prevention measures were successful because the reduced costs of damage and graffiti paid for the improvements within one year.

It was difficult to interpret the Bristol evaluation because the street lighting was gradually improved in different places over a period of 28 months. Information about crime was provided for nine successive six-month periods overlapping this time period (Shaftoe, 1994, p. 75). Therefore, the first 12-month period before the improved lighting (January-December 1986) was compared with the last 12-month period after the improved lighting (July 1989-June 1990). Table 3.5 shows the results of this comparison. Total, night-time and day-time crime decreased in the experimental area after the intervention and increased in the control area. Therefore, notwithstanding the contrary result for robbery (which was affected by small numbers in the control area), it was concluded that improved street lighting was effective in reducing crime.

In the Birmingham study of city-centre markets, there were interventions in one of the control markets that could have led to reductions in crime. Nevertheless, the reduction in thefts from the person in the experimental market after the improved lighting was far greater than in the control markets. The experimental market was large and covered, and its lighting was markedly improved. Poyner and Webb (1997, p. 89) concluded that "increased levels of illumination appear to have deterred would-be thieves".

In the Dudley study, crime was measured using before and after victim surveys in experimental and control areas. Large samples were interviewed; 431 in the experimental area and 448 in the control area. The response rate was 77 per cent in both areas. Crime decreased more in the experimental area than in the control area (Painter and Farrington, 1999a, p. 23), as shown by the interaction term in a Poisson regression equation. Furthermore, this interaction term was still significant after controlling for other predictors of crime rates including the age of the respondent (Painter and Farrington, 1997, p. 221). This type of analysis controls for prior non-comparability of the areas.

The Dudley study also evaluated the impact of improved street lighting using a self-reported delinquency survey completed by young people living on the experimental and control estates. Altogether, 307 young people were interviewed in the before survey and 334 in the after survey (Painter and Farrington, 2001a, p. 271). The self-reported delinquency results were surprisingly similar to the victim survey results. Table 3.5 shows that crimes decreased in the experimental area by 40.8 per cent according to the victim survey and by 35.0 per cent according to self-reports; crimes decreased in the control area by 15.0 per cent according to the victim survey and by 14.0 per cent according to self-reports.

The Stoke study included both adjacent and non-adjacent control areas to investigate displacement and diffusion of benefits. Again, large samples were interviewed in the victim survey; 572 before for example (an 84% response rate). The incidence of crime decreased by 42.9 per cent in the experimental area, by 45.4 per cent in the adjacent area, and by only 2.0 per cent in the control area (Painter and Farrington, 1999b, p. 97). According to interaction terms in Poisson regression equations, the changes in experimental and adjacent areas were significantly greater than in the control area. Police records showed a negligible decrease in crime of only 2 per cent in the larger police area containing all the project areas. It was concluded that improved street lighting had caused a decrease in crime in the experimental area and that there had been a diffusion of benefits to the adjacent area, which was not clearly delimited from it. It was suggested that improved street lighting might have caused increased community pride, community cohesion and informal social control, which deterred potential offenders. In Dudley and Stoke, crimes decreased both in day-time and in night-time.

Painter and Farrington (2001b) also compared the financial costs of improved street lighting with the financial benefits based on crime reduction. In Dudley, the net savings from reduced crimes in the experimental area (taking account of reductions in the control area) were 6.2 times as great as the cost of the improved street lighting. In Stoke, the savings from reduced crimes in the experimental and adjacent areas were 5.4 times as great as the cost of the improved street lighting. Therefore, in both cases, the improved street lighting more than paid for itself within one year from reduced crimes.

Table 3.6: Meta-analysis of British street lighting evaluations (odds ratios)

	Total		Violence		Property	
1. Dover (P)	1.14		..		1.14	
2. Bristol	1.35	**	0.48	*	1.57	**
3. Birmingham (P)	3.82	**	..		3.82	**
4. Dudley	1.44	**	1.76	**	1.33	**
5. Stoke-on-Trent	1.72	**	1.89	**	1.59	**
Total	1.42	**	1.41	**	1.58	**
Total (A + B)	1.25	**	1.12	*	1.19	**

Note: The odds ratio indicates the change in crimes in the control area divided by the change in crimes in the
experimental area. Odds ratios greater than 1.0 indicate a desirable effect of improved lighting.
** p<.05, * p <.10.
(P) = Available for property only.
(A + B) = American plus British data combined.

Table 3.6 presents the results of a meta-analysis of the five British projects. The Dudley figures are based on victim survey data. The odds ratios confirm the previous conclusions. Total crimes and property crimes reduced significantly after improved lighting in Bristol, Birmingham, Dudley and Stoke-on-Trent. Violent crimes reduced significantly after improved lighting in Dudley and almost significantly in Stoke-on-Trent (although they tended to increase in Bristol). While property crimes did not reduce significantly in Dover, theft of vehicles almost reduced significantly (OR = 2.87, z = 1.81, p = .07).

When the odds ratios from the five projects were combined using the methods recommended by Lipsey and Wilson (2001, p. 130), the weighted odds ratios were significant for total crimes, violent crimes and property crimes. Overall, crimes increased by 42 per cent in control areas compared with experimental areas, or conversely crimes decreased by 30 per cent in experimental areas compared with control areas. The increase was 41 per cent for violent crimes and 58 per cent for property crimes, although the violence figure was based on only three studies. The five British studies were significantly heterogeneous (Q = 18.26, 4 d.f., p = .001).

Combining the eight American and five British studies, crimes increased by 25 per cent in control areas compared with experimental areas, or conversely decreased by 20 per cent in experimental areas compared with control areas, a significant effect of improved lighting (z = 7.78, p<.0001). Property crimes increased by 19 per cent (z = 3.86, p = .0001) and violent crimes increased by 12 per cent (z = 1.70, p = .089). However, the 13 studies were significantly heterogeneous (Q = 56.91, 12 d.f., p<.0001). Both night-time and day-time crimes were measured in all five British studies; the nine night/day studies were also significantly heterogeneous (weighted odds ratio = 1.39, z = 9.43, p<.0001; Q = 25.59, 8 d.f., p=.001).

Figure 3.1: Street lighting evaluations

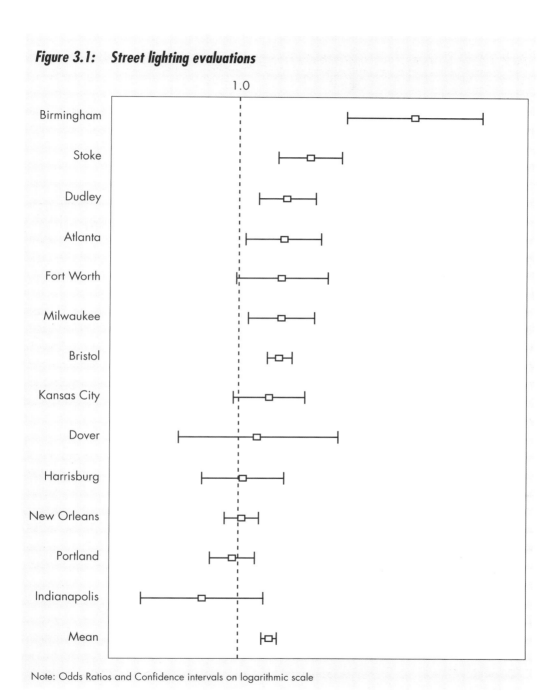

Note: Odds Ratios and Confidence intervals on logarithmic scale

Figure 3.1 summarises the results in all thirteen studies in a "Forest" graph. This shows the odds ratio for total crime in each study plus its 95 per cent confidence interval. In order to show the Birmingham study in full on the graph, logarithms of odds ratios are shown. The line indicates an odds ratio of 1.0. The 13 studies are ordered according to the magnitudes of their odds ratios. It can immediately be seen that only two studies (Portland and Indianapolis) had odds ratios less than 1, meaning that improved lighting was followed by an increase in crime, and in neither case was this increase significant. Therefore, the hypothesis that more lighting causes more crime can be firmly rejected. Furthermore, the lower confidence limit was markedly below 1 only for the last five studies, meaning that improved street lighting had a significant or near-significant effect in the desired direction in most studies. The overall weighted odds ratio of 1.25 (95% confidence interval 1.18 – 1.32) indicates the significant overall increase of 25 per cent in the crime rate in control areas compared with experimental areas in these 13 studies (a significant reduction of 20% in experimental areas).

In conclusion, these more recent British studies agree in showing that improved lighting reduces crime. They did not find that night-time crimes decreased more than day-time crimes, suggesting that a "community pride" theory may be more applicable than a "deterrence/surveillance" theory.

It would be desirable to test whether the effectiveness of street lighting in reducing crime is related to certain features of the areas studied. For example, it was speculated that improved lighting may only improve community pride in relatively stable homogeneous communities, not in areas with a heterogeneous population mix and high residential mobility. Unfortunately, insufficiently detailed information is given in the 13 studies to test this hypothesis adequately. In nevertheless attempting to test it, three studies had to be eliminated: Indianapolis because the areas were tiny (only 2-3 blocks), Dover because the "area" was a parking garage, and Birmingham because the "area" was a city-centre market.

Of the other 10 studies, Dudley and Stoke (both finding that lighting was effective) were based on stable white working class areas. Harrisburg (lighting not effective) was based on an area in transition, with Whites moving out to the suburbs and an influx of ethnic minorities. Fort Worth (effective) was based on an homogeneous (98%) Black area. Portland (not effective), Kansas City (effective) and Bristol (effective) were based on areas with large ethnic minority populations. Atlanta (effective) and New Orleans (not effective) were based on high crime areas which probably contained large ethnic minority populations, although this was not stated explicitly. Milwaukee (effective) was based on a mixed residential and commercial area adjacent to the central business district with a high percentage of older residents, so this may have been a stable area.

The lack of systematic information about residential mobility makes it difficult to draw clear conclusions about whether lighting is more effective in reducing crime in stable homogeneous communities than in unstable heterogeneous communities. Nevertheless, none of the 10 studies clearly contradicts this hypothesis, and four studies (Dudley, Stoke, Harrisburg and Fort Worth) are clearly concordant with it. The Bristol study was interesting in showing that crimes decreased most (27.4%) in an area undergoing gentrification, which is again in agreement with the hypothesis that increased community pride results in decreased crime.

4. Conclusions

Summary of main findings

The main aim of this report was to complete a systematic review of the effects of improved street lighting on crime. Rigorous methods were used to locate evidence from evaluation studies, and these methods were reported in detail. Explicit criteria were used to include or exclude studies in the review, and these criteria were also reported in detail. Sixteen potentially relevant studies were screened but excluded for various reasons, including the lack of a comparable control condition, no outcome measurement of crime and too small numbers. Key features of these studies and their results were summarised in Table 2.1. Most suggested that improved street lighting was followed by a decrease in crime.

Eight American evaluation studies met the criteria for inclusion in the review. Key features of these studies and their results were summarised in Tables 3.1 and 3.2. Their results were mixed. Four studies found that improved street lighting was effective in reducing crime, while the other four found that it was not effective. A meta-analysis found that the eight studies, taken together, showed that improved street lighting reduced crime by 7 per cent. Why the studies produced different results was not obvious, although there was a tendency for "effective" studies to measure both day-time and night-time crimes and for "ineffective" studies to measure only night-time crimes. However, all except one of these American evaluations date from the 1970s.

Five more recent British evaluation studies met the criteria for inclusion in the review. Key features of these studies and their results were summarised in Tables 3.4 and 3.5. Their results showed that improved lighting led to decreases in crime. A meta-analysis found that these five studies showed that improved lighting reduced crime by 30 per cent. The weighted effect size in all thirteen studies was substantial: a 20 per cent decrease in experimental areas compared with control areas. Furthermore, in two studies, the financial savings from reduced crimes greatly exceeded the financial costs of the improved lighting. Since these studies did not find that night-time crimes decreased more than day-time crimes, a theory of street lighting focussing on its role in increasing community pride and informal social control may be more plausible than a theory focussing on increased surveillance and increased deterrence. The results did not contradict the theory that improved lighting was most effective in reducing crime in stable homogeneous communities.

Priorities for research

Future research should be designed to test the main theories of the effects of improved street lighting (i.e. community pride versus surveillance/deterrence) more explicitly. Surveys of youth in the experimental and control areas could be carried out, to investigate their offending, their opinions of the area, their street use patterns, and factors that might inhibit them from offending (e.g. informal social control by older residents, increased surveillance after dark). Household surveys of adults could also be carried out focussing on perceptions of improvements in the community, community pride, informal social control of young people, street use and surveillance after dark.

Ideally, future research should measure crime using police records, victim surveys, and self-reports of offending. It is possible that one effect of improved street lighting may be to facilitate or encourage reporting of crimes to the police, for example if victims get a better view of offenders. The surveys of potential victims and potential offenders are necessary for testing key hypotheses about the effects of improved lighting.

Future research should ideally include several experimental areas and several comparable adjacent and control areas. Adjacent areas are needed to test hypotheses about displacement and diffusion of benefits. The comparability of experimental, adjacent and control areas should be investigated. The use of several areas would make it more possible to establish boundary conditions under which improved lighting had greater or lesser effects. The numbers of crimes recorded in each area in the pretest should be sufficient to detect changes reliably (as indicated by a statistical power analysis). Ideally, large numbers of potential victims and potential offenders should be surveyed.

Crimes should be measured before and after the intervention in experimental, adjacent and control areas. Ideally, a long time series of crimes should be studied, to investigate pre-existing crime trends and also how far any effects of street lighting persist or wear off over time. This would also help to determine how far a decrease in crime after a high rate might reflect regression to the mean. Different types of crimes should be measured, and also crimes committed during day-time and the hours of darkness. The improvement in lighting in different areas should be carefully measured, including vertical and horizontal levels of illumination. Cost-benefit analyses of the impact of improved street lighting should be carried out.

Most importantly, systematic information should be collected and reported in each evaluation project about such topics as the dates of the research and of the interventions, the design of the study, characteristics of areas, hypotheses to be tested, operational definitions of variables, implementation issues, events occurring over time in all areas, lengths of before and after measurement periods, numbers of crimes, strength of effects and statistical significance of results, and financial costs and benefits. It is important to specify characteristics of areas in order to investigate external validity, or what works with whom in what settings. Systematic reviews in the future would be easier to carry out if each project followed a checklist of topics to be covered. This applies to all types of criminological evaluations.

Finally, in testing hypotheses, it would be useful to investigate the effects of street lighting in conjunction with other crime prevention interventions. To the extent that community pride is important, this could be enhanced by other environmental improvements. To the extent that surveillance is important, this could be enhanced by other interventions such as closed-circuit television cameras. For example, one experimental area could have both improved street lighting and CCTV, a second could have only improved street lighting, and a third could have only CCTV. This kind of planned evaluation of interactions of crime prevention initiatives has rarely been attempted before.

Policy implications

The policy implications of research on improved street lighting have been well articulated by Pease (1999). He pointed out that situational crime prevention involves the modification of environments so that crimes involve more effort, more risk and lower rewards. The first step in any crime reduction programme requires a careful analysis of situations and how they affect potential offenders and potential victims. The second step involves implementing crime reduction interventions. Whether improved street lighting is likely to be effective in reducing crime would depend on characteristics of situations and on other concurrent situational interventions. Efforts to reduce crime should take account of the fact that crime tends to be concentrated among certain people and in certain locations, rather than being evenly distributed throughout a community.

The British studies included in this review show that improved street lighting can be effective in reducing crime in some circumstances. Exactly what are the optimal circumstances is not clear at present, and this needs to be established by future evaluation research. However, it is clear that improved street lighting should be considered as a potential strategy in any crime reduction programme in coordination with other intervention strategies. Depending on the analysis of the crime problem, improved street lighting could often be implemented as a feasible, inexpensive and effective method of reducing crime.

Street lighting has some advantages over other situational measures which have been associated with the creeping privatisation of public space, the exclusion of sections of the population and the move towards a "fortress" society (Bottoms, 1990). Street lighting benefits the whole neighbourhood rather than particular individuals or households. It is not a physical barrier to crime, it has no adverse civil liberties implications and it can increase public safety and effective use of neighbourhood streets at night. In short, improved street lighting seems to have no negative effects and demonstrated benefits for law-abiding citizens.

Appendix 1: Literature reviews consulted

The following eight literature reviews were consulted as part of the search strategies used to identify evaluation reports on the effects of improved street lighting on crime.

Eck, J. E. (1997). Preventing crime at places. In L. W. Sherman, D. C. Gottfredson, D.L. MacKenzie, J. E. Eck, P. Reuter and S. D. Bushway, (eds.) *Preventing Crime: What Works, What Doesn't, What's Promising* (ch. 7). Washington, D.C.: National Institute of Justice, U.S. Department of Justice.

Eck, J. E. (2002). Preventing crime at places. In L. W. Sherman, D. P. Farrington, B. C. Welsh and D.L. MacKenzie (eds.) *Evidence-Based Crime Prevention.* (pp. 241-294). London: Routledge.

Fleming, R. and Burrows, J. (1986). The case for lighting as a means of preventing crime. *Home Office Research Bulletin*, 22, 14-17.

Painter, K. A. (1996). Street lighting, crime and fear of crime: A summary of research. In T. H. Bennett (ed.) *Preventing Crime and Disorder: Targeting Strategies and Responsibilities* (pp. 313-351). Cambridge: Institute of Criminology, University of Cambridge.

Pease, K. (1999). A review of street lighting evaluations: Crime reduction effects. In K. A. Painter and N. Tilley (eds.) *Surveillance of Public Space: CCTV, Street Lighting and Crime Prevention* (pp. 47-76). Monsey, N.Y.: Criminal Justice Press.

Poyner, B. (1993). What works in crime prevention: An overview of evaluations. In R.V. Clarke (ed.) *Crime Prevention Studies*, Vol. 1 (pp. 7-34). Monsey, N.Y.: Criminal Justice Press.

Ramsay, M. and Newton, R. (1991). *The Effect of Better Street Lighting on Crime and Fear: A Review.* (Crime Prevention Unit Paper 29.) London: Home Office.

Tien, J. M., O'Donnell, V. F., Barnett, A. and Mirchandani, P. B. (1979). *Street Lighting Projects: National Evaluation Program, Phase 1 Report.* Washington, D.C.: National Institute of Law Enforcement and Criminal Justice, U.S. Department of Justice.

Appendix 2: Evaluation reports that could not be obtained

The following four evaluation reports were identified by Tien et al. (1979), but copies could not be obtained. (James Tien and Arnold Barnett, as well as U.S. government sources were contacted.)

Department of Public Works (1976). *A Brief Update on 'Miami Relights'*. (July). Miami, Florida: Author.

Denver Anti-Crime Council (1977). *Final Report: Street Lighting Project*. (June). Unpublished draft. Denver, Colorado: Author.

Newark High Impact Evaluation Staff (1975). *Street Lighting Project Interim Evaluation Report*. (December). Newark, N.J.: Author.

Tucson Department of Human and Community Development (1971). *First Action Year: August 1, 1970-July 31, 1971. Project Evaluation Report*. (October). Tucson, Arizona: Author.

It is not known if these reports would meet the inclusion criteria. According to Tien et al. (1979), the control area was the city for the Miami and Newark projects, so they would likely be excluded. However, according to Tien *et al.* (1979), Denver had an adjacent control area and Tucson had randomly selected experimental and control areas, so they might be evaluation projects that should be included.

The following evaluation report was identified by Ramsay and Newton (1991), but could not be obtained. (Malcolm Ramsay was contacted.)

Vamplew, C. (1990). *The Effect of Improved Street Lighting on Perceptions of Crime: A Before-and-After Study*. Cleveland County Council, Research and Intelligence Unit.

From the description given by Ramsay and Newton (1991), it is unclear whether the experimental and control areas in this study are comparable.

References

Angel, S. (1968). *Discouraging Crime Through City Planning.* (Working Paper No. 5.) Berkeley, California: University of California.

Atkins, S., Husain, S. and Storey, A. (1991). *The Influence of Street Lighting on Crime and Fear of Crime* (Crime Prevention Unit Paper 28). London: Home Office.

Atlanta Regional Commission (1974). *Street Light Project: Final Evaluation Report.* Atlanta, Georgia: Author.

Bachner, J. P. (1985). Effective security lighting. *Journal of Security Administration, 9,* 59-67.

Barr, R. and Pease, K. (1990). Crime placement, displacement and deflection. In M. Tonry and N. Morris (eds.) *Crime and Justice,* Vol. 12 (pp. 277-318). Chicago, Illinois: University of Chicago Press.

Bennett, T. H. and Wright, R. (1984). *Burglars on Burglary.* Farnborough, Hants: Gower.

Bottoms, A. E. (1990). Crime prevention facing the 1990s. *Policing and Society, 1,* 3-22.

Challinger, D. (1992). Less telephone vandalism: How did it happen? In R. V. Clarke (ed.) *Situational Crime Prevention: Successful Case Studies* (pp. 75-88). Albany, N.Y.: Harrow and Heston.

Clarke, R. V. (1995). Situational crime prevention. In M. Tonry and D. P. Farrington (eds.) *Building a Safer Society: Strategic Approaches to Crime Prevention* (pp. 91-150). Chicago, Illinois: University of Chicago Press.

Clarke, R. V. and Weisburd, D. (1994). Diffusion of crime control benefits: Observations on the reverse of displacement. In R. V. Clarke (ed.) *Crime Prevention Studies,* Vol. 2 (pp. 165-183). Monsey, N.Y.: Criminal Justice Press.

Cohen, L. E. and Felson, M. (1979). Social change and crime rate trends: A routine activity approach. *American Sociological Review, 44,* 588-608.

Cook, T. D. and Campbell, D. T. (1979). *Quasi-Experimentation: Design and Analysis Issues for Field Settings.* Chicago, Illinois: Rand McNally.

Davidson, N. and Goodey, J. (1991). *Final Report of the Hull Street Lighting and Crime Project.* Hull: School of Geography and Earth Sciences, University of Hull.

Department of Intergovernmental Fiscal Liaison (1973). *Preliminary Report – Milwaukee High Intensity Street Lighting Project.* Milwaukee, Wisconsin.: Author.

Department of Intergovernmental Fiscal Liaison (1974). *Final Report – Milwaukee High Intensity Street Lighting Project.* Milwaukee, Wisconsin: Author.

Ditton, J. and Nair, G. (1994). Throwing light on crime: A study of the relationship between street lighting and crime prevention. *Security Journal, 5,* 125-132.

Farrington, D. P. (1983). Randomized experiments on crime and justice. In M.Tonry and N. Morris (eds.) *Crime and Justice,* Vol. 4 (pp. 257-308). Chicago, Illinois: University of Chicago Press.

Farrington, D. P. (1997). Evaluating a community crime prevention program. *Evaluation, 3,* 157-173.

Farrington, D. P. and Petrosino, A. (2000). Systematic reviews of criminological interventions: The Campbell Collaboration Crime and Justice Group. *International Annals of Criminology, 38,* 49-66.

Farrington, D. P. and Petrosino, A. (2001). The Campbell Collaboration Crime and Justice Group. *Annals of the American Academy of Political and Social Science, 578,* 35-49.

Fleming, R. and Burrows, J. (1986). The case for lighting as a means of preventing crime. *Home Office Research Bulletin, 22,* 14-17.

Griswold, D. B. (1984). Crime prevention and commercial burglary: A time series analysis. *Journal of Criminal Justice, 12,* 493-501.

Hack, G. (1974). *Improving City Streets for Use at Night: The Norfolk Experiment.* Norfolk, Virginia: Norfolk Redevelopment and Housing Authority.

Harrisburg Police Department (1976). *Final Evaluation Report of the "High Intensity Street Lighting Program"*. Harrisburg, Pennsylvania: Planning and Research Section, Staff and Technical Services Division, Harrisburg Police Department.

Inskeep, N. R. and Goff, C. (1974). *A Preliminary Evaluation of the Portland Lighting Project*. Salem, Oregon: Oregon Law Enforcement Council.

Jacobs, J. (1961). *The Death and Life of Great American Cities*. New York: Random House.

Krause, P. B. (1977). The impact of high intensity street lighting on night-time business burglary. *Human Factors, 19*, 235-239.

Kushmuk, J. and Whittemore, S. L. (1981). *A Re-evaluation of Crime Prevention through Environmental Design Program in Portland, Oregon: Executive Summary*. Washington, D.C.: National Institute of Justice, U.S. Department of Justice.

La Vigne, N. G. (1994). Gasoline drive-offs: Designing a less convenient environment. In R. V. Clarke (ed.) *Crime Prevention Studies*, Vol. 2 (pp. 91-114). Monsey, N.Y.: Criminal Justice Press.

Lavrakas, P. J. and Kushmuk, J. W. (1986). Evaluating crime prevention through environmental design: The Portland commercial demonstration project. In D. P. Rosenbaum (ed.) *Community Crime Prevention: Does It Work?* (pp. 202-227). Beverly Hills, California: Sage.

Lewis, E. B. and Sullivan, T. T. (1979). Combating crime and citizen attitudes: A case study of the corresponding reality. *Journal of Criminal Justice, 7*, 71-79.

Lipsey, M. W. and Wilson, D. B. (2001). *Practical Meta-Analysis*. Thousand Oaks, California: Sage.

Mayhew, P., Clarke, R. V., Burrows, J. N., Hough, J. M. and Winchester, S. W. C. (1979). *Crime in Public View*. (Home Office Research Study 40.) London: Her Majesty's Stationery Office.

Nair, G., Ditton, J. and Phillips, S. (1993). Environmental improvements and the fear of crime: The sad case of the 'pond' area in Glasgow. *British Journal of Criminology, 33*, 555-561.

Nair, G., McNair, D. G. and Ditton, J. (1997). Street lighting: Unexpected benefits to young pedestrians from improvement. *Lighting Research and Technology, 29*, 143-149.

Newman, O. (1972). *Defensible Space: Crime Prevention Through Urban Design*. New York: Macmillan.

Painter, K. A. (1994). The impact of street lighting on crime, fear, and pedestrian street use. *Security Journal*, 5, 116-124.

Painter, K. A. (1996). Street lighting, crime and fear of crime: A summary of research. In T. H. Bennett (ed.) *Preventing Crime and Disorder: Targeting Strategies and Responsibilities* (pp. 313-351). Cambridge: Institute of Criminology, University of Cambridge.

Painter, K. A. and Farrington, D. P. (1997). The crime reducing effect of improved street lighting: The Dudley project. In R. V. Clarke (ed.) *Situational Crime Prevention: Successful Case Studies*, 2nd ed. (pp. 209-226). Guilderland, N.Y.: Harrow and Heston.

Painter, K. A. and Farrington, D. P. (1999a). Improved street lighting: Crime reducing effects and cost-benefit analyses. *Security Journal*, 12, 17-32.

Painter, K. A. and Farrington, D. P. (1999b). Street lighting and crime: Diffusion of benefits in the Stoke-on-Trent project. In K. A. Painter & N. Tilley (eds.) *Surveillance of Public Space: CCTV, Street Lighting and Crime Prevention* (pp. 77-122). Monsey, N.Y.: Criminal Justice Press.

Painter, K. A. and Farrington, D. P. (2001a). Evaluating situational crime prevention using a young people's survey. *British Journal of Criminology*, 41, 266-284.

Painter, K. A. and Farrington, D. P. (2001b). The financial benefits of improved street lighting, based on crime reduction. *Lighting Research and Technology*, 33, 3-12.

Pease, K. (1999). A review of street lighting evaluations: Crime reduction effects. In K. A. Painter and N. Tilley (eds.) *Surveillance of Public Space: CCTV, Street Lighting and Crime Prevention* (pp. 47-76). Monsey, N.Y.: Criminal Justice Press.

Petrosino, A., Turpin-Petrosino, C. and Finckenauer, J. O. (2000). Well-meaning programs can have harmful effects! Lessons from experiments of programs such as Scared Straight. *Crime and Delinquency*, 46, 354-379.

Poyner, B. (1991). Situational crime prevention in two parking facilities. *Security Journal*, 2, 96-101.

Poyner, B. and Webb, B. (1997). Reducing theft from shopping bags in city centre markets. In R. V. Clarke (ed.) *Situational Crime Prevention: Successful Case Studies,* 2nd ed. (pp. 83-89). Guilderland, N.Y.: Harrow and Heston.

Quinet, K. D. and Nunn, S. (1998). Illuminating crime: The impact of street lighting on calls for police service. *Evaluation Review, 22, 751-779.*

Ramsay, M. and Newton, R. (1991). *The Effect of Better Street Lighting on Crime and Fear: A Review.* (Crime Prevention Unit Paper 29.) London: Home Office.

Reppetto, T. A. (1976). Crime prevention and the displacement phenomenon. *Crime and Delinquency, 22, 166-177.*

Shaftoe, H. (1994). Easton/Ashley, Bristol: Lighting improvements. In S. Osborn (ed.) *Housing Safe Communities: An Evaluation of Recent Initiatives* (pp. 72-77). London: Safe Neighbourhoods Unit.

Sherman, L. W. and Weisburd, D. (1995). General deterrent effects of police patrol in crime "hot spots": A randomized controlled trial. *Justice Quarterly,* 12, 625-648.

Siemon, J. M. and Vardell, L. (1974). A bright answer to the crime and energy question. *Police Chief,* June, 53-55.

Skogan, W. G. (1990). *Disorder and Decline: Crime and the Spiral of Decay in American Neighborhoods.* New York: Free Press.

Sternhell, R. (1977). *The Limits of Lighting: The New Orleans Experiment in Crime Reduction: Final Impact Evaluation Report.* New Orleans, Louisiana: Mayor's Criminal Justice Coordinating Council.

Taub, R. P., Taylor, D. G. and Dunham, J. D. (1984). *Paths of Neighborhood Change: Race and Crime in Urban America.* Chicago, Illinois: University of Chicago Press.

Taylor, R. B. and Gottfredson, S. (1986). Environmental design, crime and prevention: An examination of community dynamics. In A. J. Reiss and M. Tonry (eds.) *Communities and Crime* (pp. 387-416). Chicago: University of Chicago Press.

Tien, J. M., O'Donnell, V. F., Barnett, A. and Mirchandani, P. B. (1979). *Street Lighting Projects: National Evaluation Program, Phase 1 Report.* Washington, D.C.: National Institute of Law Enforcement and Criminal Justice, U.S. Department of Justice.

Tilley, N. (1993). *The Prevention of Crime against Small Businesses: The Safer Cities Experience.* (Crime Prevention Unit Paper 45.) London: Home Office.

Vrij, A. and Winkel, F. W. (1991). Characteristics of the built environment and fear of crime: A research note on interventions in unsafe locations. *Deviant Behavior,* 12, 203-215.

Warr, M. (1990). Dangerous situations: Social context and fear of victimization. *Social Forces,* 68, 891-907.

Wilson, J. Q. and Kelling, G. L. (1982). Broken windows. *The Atlantic Monthly* (March), 29-38.

Wright, R., Heilweil, M., Pelletier, P. and Dickinson, K. (1974). *The Impact of Street Lighting on Crime.* Ann Arbor, Michigan: University of Michigan.

RDS Publications

Requests for Publications

Copies of our publications and a list of those currently available may be obtained from:

> Home Office
> Research, Development and Statistics Directorate
> Communication Development Unit
> Room 275, Home Office
> 50 Queen Anne's Gate
> London SW1H 9AT
> Telephone: 020 7273 2084 (answerphone outside of office hours)
> Facsimile: 020 7222 0211
> E-mail: publications.rds@homeoffice.gsi.gov.uk

alternatively

why not visit the RDS web-site at
>   Internet: http://www.homeoffice.gov.uk/rds/index.htm

where many of our publications are available to be read on screen or downloaded for printing.